GET YOURSELF
ELECTED

GET YOURSELF ELECTED

Quick Tips for Winning a Local Election

Tammy Pickering Barnett

OPEN BOOK EDITIONS
A Beorts-Kosher Partner

iUniverse®

GET YOURSELF ELECTED
QUICK TIPS FOR WINNING A LOCAL ELECTION

Disclaimer of Warranty/Limitation of Liability
The publisher and author have used their best efforts in preparing this material. The publisher and author make no representations or warranties with respect to the accuracy or completeness of the contents of this work, and specifically disclaim any implied warranties of merchantability or fitness for a particular purpose. There are no warranties that extend beyond the descriptions contained in this paragraph. Neither the publisher nor author shall be liable for any damages arising from the use of the book's information, including without limitation actual, special, incidental, consequential, or other damages. This work is sold with the understanding that the publisher and author are not engaged in rendering legal, accounting, or other professional services. If professional assistance is required, the services of a competent professional should be obtained. Neither the publisher nor the author shall be liable for damages arising herefrom. References to an organization or website in this work as a citation and/or a potential source for further information does not mean the publisher or author endorses the information the organization or website may provide or recommendations it may make. The resources listed in this work are for information purposes only, not endorsements or referrals, and neither publisher nor author shall be liable or responsible for any loss or damage experienced in dealing with any such listed resources or providers. Readers should be aware that Internet websites listed in this work may have changed or no longer be available between the time this work was written and when it is read by the reader.

To protect people's privacy, names have been omitted in the examples included in this work.

iUniverse books may be ordered through booksellers or by contacting:

iUniverse
1663 Liberty Drive
Bloomington, IN 47403
www.iuniverse.com
1-800-Authors (1-800-288-4677)

Because of the dynamic nature of the Internet, any web addresses or links contained in this book may have changed since publication and may no longer be valid. The views expressed in this work are solely those of the author and do not necessarily reflect the views of the publisher, and the publisher hereby disclaims any responsibility for them.

Any people depicted in stock imagery provided by Thinkstock are models, and such images are being used for illustrative purposes only.
Certain stock imagery © Thinkstock.

ISBN: 978-1-4917-6190-8 (sc)
ISBN: 978-1-4917-6189-2 (hc)
ISBN: 978-1-4917-6191-5 (e)

Library of Congress Control Number: 2015903134

Print information available on the last page.

iUniverse rev. date: 03/26/2015

Thank you to my campaign manager, Lezlie Simmons, who went above and beyond the call of duty, and to family and friends who provided much support during the campaign—Toni Ann, Ryan, Greg, Stephanie, Steve, Tom, my mom and dad, Patty, and Tonda.

Contents

Introduction

Learn from the mistakes of others. You can't live long enough to make them all yourself.
—Eleanor Roosevelt

The purpose of this book is to share the tips I learned with those new to campaigning for local office. It's written for candidates and their key team members and includes tips on what to watch for in the process, from deciding whether or not to run, to understanding the politics within the politics of city and county elections.

These are tips I learned while campaigning for an at-large county council seat after chairing the Get-Out-the-Vote campaign for the Vanderburgh Democratic Party in Evansville, Indiana, during two elections. One of those campaigns was during the election of US Rep. Brad Ellsworth, whose race in the hotly contested Eight Congressional District was one of the first ones called by the cable news networks. By running my own campaign and also volunteering for local and state campaigns, I learned the ins and outs of political campaigning at the local level.

The examples shared in this book are from actual local campaigns. Candidates' names and specific community references have been omitted to protect people's privacy.

How to use this book

This book is not intended as a manual but instead as a quick way to review tips that you can apply to a political campaign for a local elected office. It's divided into categories that comprise main areas involved in running a campaign, mainly how to develop your message and equip your team with the tools to help get the message out to voters so they'll know why you're the candidate who deserves their vote.

Chapter 1 reviews the importance of finding out the political landscape of your community at the outset of your campaign. This information is good background information to consider as you build your campaign.

The next two chapters cover what's needed for the backbone of your campaign: developing your message and your campaign strategy. Tips for building a strong campaign team and solid volunteer base are shared in chapters 4 and 5.

The next chapter on getting organized gives you personal tips to work more efficiently and as stress-free as possible. Chapters on raising funds, getting your name out, and building a volunteer base prepare you for the main goal of your campaign, Getting Out the Vote.

Chapter 10 covers specific tips for how to maximize the vote turnout. As a female candidate and one of the co-founders of the Vanderburgh County Democratic Women's Caucus, I've seen female candidates face challenges in political campaigns. Chapter 11 includes tips and advice from female candidates and officeholders in Indiana. Each chapter includes questions and action items to help you think through the information and decide how to apply it to your campaign.

Many of the tips center on things you can begin planning before the start of your campaign. Much of what happens during a campaign is unexpected, such as the entry of a new opponent into the race or a surprise question from a voter during a debate. So it's good to concentrate on what you have more control over. You'll then be better prepared to think on your feet for those unscripted and unexpected moments on the campaign trail.

Orientation to the
Political Landscape

A political landscape is the combination of the political culture and history of your community. Are there families who have been involved in the local government for years? Are there past races that caused rifts in your local party? Have there been newcomers who ran for office in the past? If so, how were they received by the political and community leaders? Who are the main players, and what are the unwritten rules? And it goes without saying that the unwritten ones are the trickiest. What's going on behind the scene? You won't be able to know everything right away or even after your campaign, but by meeting with key political stakeholders in your community, you'll have a head start that may help you avoid a misstep. These leaders may be those holding offices now or people who once did but are now retired and active in mentoring. So no matter what office you're seeking, take the time to meet with political leaders (both official and unofficial) before campaign season. The tips that follow give you specific ways to learn and understand the political background and makeup of your community.

Take calculated risks. This is quite different from being rash.
—US Army General George S. Patton

The political landscape can affect your campaign in many ways. For example, you can run into pressure from a political party or leaders in your community. Some might encourage you to enter another race or change your timing or alter your focus or support of an issue. *Always remember that it's your name on the line and that you've got to stay true to your values and personal mission.* I've heard people say that they were looking for someone to run in a particular race either to make the opposing party or candidate spend money or to help the party look competitive. That might be true, but don't fall for it. You should run for office only if, after careful research and consultation with others in your community, you believe you have a reasonably good chance of winning the race. Because you'll be asking people to give their time and money to your campaign, you want to be sure that your campaign has a good chance of success.

1. **Attend the meetings of the office for which you are seeking.**

    This gives you a chance to see firsthand how business is conducted, along with the challenges and opportunities of the office. Check to see if your community's public broadcasting channel or other public access channel films the meetings and rebroadcasts them. You can then check the viewing schedule and record them to view at your convenience. You could also read the minutes of the meeting, which should be part of public record. Many communities provide links to the meeting files on their websites. (If this is not occurring yet in your community, this could be something you suggest during your campaign as a way to make the office more transparent and accountable to the public.)

2. **Know the duties, responsibilities, and scope of the office you are seeking.**

    This sounds simple, but it's often what trips candidates up when answering questions from the media and during a debate.

Understanding exactly what the position entails will help you educate voters on what can be done and what falls outside the scope of the office. For example, if you are passionate about the maintenance of community parks, but its budget is controlled by another office, you'll know that this isn't an issue to be addressed by your campaign. To get this information, first check with your county's election office to learn where to obtain the specific listing of the duties and tasks of the position. Many states also have an association of counties that provides information and training for specific county elected offices.

Sample key questions to research:

What is the main objective of that office?

What are the basic duties? The responsibilities and tasks for local elected offices are spelled out in the municipal code for your town or county. Visit your local government's website and also refer to Votesmart.org for this information.

What are the minimum qualifications for the position?

Is this office a full-time or part-time commitment?

What is the salary paid to the officeholder?

What is the budget for that office (or board or department)?

Are there employees that report to this officeholder? If so, what are their positions?

Your list of questions will be much longer, but you can use these to get started.

3. **One of your first visits should be to the chair of your local political party if you are running in a partisan election.**

   Remember the adage that you don't want to surprise your allies. You will need their support, and by calling on them first before making your campaign official, you'll let them know that you recognize and appreciate the importance of their role.

   If you are running in a nonpartisan race, visit the chairs of both political parties to ask for support and seek advice even if you tend to identify with a specific party personally. Many voters who identify themselves with a political party are independent minded when it comes to voting for local offices, so keep your options open and reach out to both parties if you are not running under a party affiliation.

4. **Volunteer for a local campaign.**

   You'll see a campaign from the inside out and make contacts for your campaign. It also helps you gain recognition with others in the party. Be sure to take notes! There's no sense in starting from scratch. In my community, it's almost a rite of passage for people to work on at least one campaign if not several before launching their own campaign. They gain knowledge on how to run a campaign, seeing things that they'll adopt and things they'll choose not to do based on the trial and error of others' campaigns. Plus, they are depositing favors in the bank for when they decide to run.

   Be selective as far as which candidates you decide to give your time to. Before making your choice, plan to meet with several candidates to get to know their missions and their individual styles so you'll have a better feel as to how they'll run their campaign. You want to work for someone whose values align with your own and who is well organized. The person should be confident enough in themselves and in you to give you a chance to work in different areas within the campaign so you can have a well-rounded experience. Then, be sure to spell out up front the time you have available.

I let the candidate I chose to volunteer for know up front that one reason I was volunteering my time was to learn all I could for my own future campaign. I was fortunate that the person I worked for was gracious and very open to sharing not only responsibilities and opportunities to build my skills but also the details and reasons behind decisions made during his campaign.

5. **Meet with past candidates for the office you are seeking.**

Contact past candidates individually, extending an invitation to meet for coffee, breakfast, or lunch (depending on your budget). Talk with candidates who were not successful in their bid for the office, as well as those who won the race. Ask them if they would be willing to share their experiences, including what went well during the campaign and what they would do differently. Ask them for advice. More than likely, they will be flattered that you acknowledge their experience. Be sure to follow up your meeting with a handwritten thank-you card.

If you don't remember who ran in past campaigns, research this information by accessing your community newspaper's online archives. You could also check with the county clerk or official in charge of elections. The local Democratic or Republican headquarters is another resource to check for information on past candidates.

6. **Seek opportunities for candidate training programs in your community.**

During the year I ran, the Chamber of Commerce partnered with the local public university to provide a one-day program that was reasonably priced and gave potential candidates a chance to pose questions to the media, election officials, officeholders, and past candidates. Other sources for training include your local party. Besides providing valuable tips and resources, it also gives you a chance to meet other candidates you can connect with during your campaign.

During the training session, I met several candidates that I kept in touch with during the campaign cycle. One particular candidate was running for a similar office in the neighboring county. We continued to see each other at events. It was nice to see a friendly face at events and to have someone I knew would understand my concerns firsthand.

Also ask your local party chair if any candidate mentoring programs are planned. During my campaign, our local party organized orientation and training for all candidates using a lunch and learn format. Each of these meetings featured information on a city department. The department head or someone from that office gave a brief presentation on the department's overall mission and status. They also shared their goals and challenges and gave us a chance to ask questions. These sessions were well attended and very beneficial for candidates, especially those new to local government. Thanks to the program, we had a better understanding of the inner workings of local government and a greater appreciation for the budgeting challenges they faced and how our elected office might impact the individual departments that make up the local government.

By having an opportunity to meet the department managers and employees one-on-one, we felt more comfortable calling on them if needed during the course of our campaigns. Plus, it gave us a chance to build relationships with the other candidates.

If there aren't any training opportunities provided locally, call the closest community college or adult education center to suggest they offer one.

7. **Contact local officeholders to ask if you can drop by and visit them at their office to learn more about their concerns.**

Your office will work with many local officeholders, so it's good to meet these individuals to introduce yourself and build goodwill. Prepare for the meeting as you would for a job interview. In some sense it is an interview because you're hoping you'll make a good impression on them and begin building a connection that will be helpful during the campaign and then also afterward once you're elected. That means doing your research on the office or department's key functions and duties. Develop a few questions to ask the officeholder. Make these open-ended questions to give them a chance to share their experiences with you.

For example:

"What is the biggest challenge this office has faced this year?"

"What accomplishment are you most proud of?"

"How has the working relationship been with the person in the office I'm seeking?"

"Do you see areas in which the relationship could be improved?"

Be careful to state these last two questions in a manner so that the person understands you're not asking him/her to criticize anyone, that you merely want to obtain ideas for continuous improvement.

While there, ask if they will introduce you to their staff. Treat this visit like you would any other campaign stop. You'll want to be sure to give them information on your background, why you're running for office, and what you plan to do if elected.

If it's within your budget, leave pens and notepads imprinted with your campaign message. This will keep your name in the office. And, of course, be sure to mail a handwritten thank-you note to the manager of each office.

Questions

1. Who are three people in your community you can ask about the political landscape in your town? What are at least two questions you plan to ask them?

2. Which task or responsibility of the office you're seeking excites you most?

Actions

1. Research the scope of the office you're seeking. Find the statute that spells out the duties and qualifications of the office.

2. Meet with the chair of the local party or both parties if you're running in a nonpartisan race.

3. Call the Chamber of Commerce and community colleges to find a candidate training program to attend.

CHAPTER 2

Developing Your Message

One of the first things voters will want to know is the reason you're running. Your answer should include the vision you have for your community and the goals for making that vision a reality. Your message should set you apart from your opponents and clearly define what improvements you want to give to voters. Remember, it's not only about defining who you are as a candidate, but also defining yourself in terms of what you can do to improve the lives of people in your community. So your message needs to answer: what's in it for them? Why do you deserve their vote? The following tips will help you refine your message.

1. **Research your community so you can answer the following questions no matter which local office you are seeking.**

    Population of your city or county:

    The total city or county budget:

    What is the local government's average annual revenue?

    Who are the main employers?

What is the unemployment rate?

Which issues most affect your community? Is the unemployment rate high? Are there environmental issues specific to your town or region? Pay special attention to the editorials and letters to the editor. Watch the local news broadcasts. Then, identify which of these issues you'll be able to impact in the office you're seeking.

You'll want to be specific about how an issue that might be cast as a national issue, such as healthcare reform, can be impacted by local government. If it cannot be impacted at the local level, this would not be an issue to develop for a local race.

This is important to keep in mind. Thus, if you've been passionate about politics and have followed the national issues, be sure to localize them. If you're concerned about healthcare reform, unless there is a local tie-on or a way the local office you're seeking will be able to impact this issue, spend your energy instead on issues that are closely related and can be influenced at the local level. For example, in our county, the commissioners researched and introduced a community medical prescription card. The free card is available to all county residents and can help them save money on prescription medicine just by virtue of being a county resident and showing the card to the pharmacist. It was a good way to address a national issue with something practical that people could do to save money.

Another national issue on voters' radar the year I ran was the Iraq War. This was an issue that definitely had affected our community since local men and women were stationed there. However, since this was not an issue that could be decided upon by local government offices, local candidates didn't spend much time talking about their positions on the war. Instead, they highlighted those issues that could be impacted locally.

All politics is local.
—Thomas P. (Tip) O'Neill Jr., Speaker of the House

Main Issues of Voters in Your community

Issue #1 is _____

How is this impacted at the local level? _____

_____

Issue #2 is _____

How is this impacted at the local level? _____

_____

Issue #3 is _____

How is this impacted at the local level? _____

_____

---

2. **Identify what your top three priorities will be if you are elected.**

   An example would be to increase public safety, bring new jobs to the area, and eliminate waste to save taxpayers' money. Three is a good number because it's easy for you to remember, and it's easier to keep your message succinct for voters. My three-point message shown below was printed on hard-stock paper and was included with fundraising materials and as handouts at community events.

**My Key Initiatives for a Brighter
Future for Our Community**

- **Attractive, Sustainable, Innovative and Healthier
  Community**

  Seek, encourage and incentivize innovative businesses that
  offer good jobs in the community and are good citizens
  (emphasizing green building and processes).

  Ensure the main gateways to our county reflect a welcoming,
  positive image.

  Collaborate to extend greenways and biking pathways and
  other outdoor activity areas throughout the county.

- **Sound Fiscal Practices for County Government**

  Make Appropriate and Effective Use of Tax Dollars.

  Provide Good Value to the Citizens of the Community.

  Find Ways to Make Local Government More Efficient.

- **Open and Accessible County Government**

  Ensure convenient and accessible Council meetings that
  enable greater attendance and participation by the community.

  Use the county's website and other easily accessible avenues
  to provide more information on the workings of county
  government, including advanced detailed agendas and use of
  the website to facilitate more input and feedback from citizens.

For a quick reply to interviewers, those were condensed into the following points:

1. Develop collaborative community initiatives for an attractive and healthier community
2. Work with county council members to implement sound fiscal practices for county government
3. Promote an open and accessible county government

3. **Know your competition.**

Research your opponent's background and position on the issues important to your community. To do this, use Google or other search engines to locate articles and editorials about the officeholder's performance in office. A reference librarian at your community or university library can also help you. You want to find out what message they are communicating. How are they trying to appeal to voters? The more you know about the opposition, the better prepared you will be to distinguish yourself from the competition and fine-tune your message to voters accordingly.

4. **Write a biography summarizing your background and emphasizing the experiences, training, and credentials that make you uniquely qualified to hold the office.**

The biography or bio can be posted on your campaign website and also sent to the press. And you may be asked to give one to community groups hosting candidate nights. Your bio should also include details about your ties to the community. You want voters to know that you are one of them and that you share their values and passion for improving the community.

Don't assume voters will know the responsibilities of the office you're seeking. Local government can be confusing, especially in communities where voters participate in both county and city elections. My campaign material included a brief explanation of the role of county council in our local government. See the following example.

The Job of County Council

- Fiscal control over county offices, boards, departments and commissions
- Approves all job descriptions, salaries, and staffing limits for offices, boards, departments, and commissions funded by the county
- Fixes the tax rate and levy for the county
- Considers and votes on all county tax abatements
- Makes appointments as provided by ordinance law

There are seven (7) County Council Members. Three of them are at-large (county wide), and four are elected by district.

---

5. **Create an elevator pitch.**

It's a short statement that will include your full name, the office you're seeking, and why you decided to run. That might seem like a long paragraph. However, so that it will fit into the time it takes to introduce yourself in an elevator, keep it under ten seconds. Here are a couple of examples:

I'm Tammy Barnett, and I'm running for county council to make county government more accessible and accountable to the public it serves.

I'm Bill Smith, and I'm running for county auditor to ensure all citizens receive a fair and accurate assessment of their property.

6. **Stay updated on the local issues impacting your community.**

This will help you better prepare for debates and question-and-answer sessions at candidate forums. Also, tune into the local radio and television news to see the issues being covered.

7. **Be succinct in your debate responses and media interviews.**

Work on your presentation skills. It's one of the most important skills for candidates to develop and practice. Realize that the more you speak the more comfortable you'll become and the more effective you'll be able to communicate.

Respond to questions with a succinct answer and then *stop talking*. So often, candidates start out strong, but rather than ending on a strong note, they run out of things to say *before* they stop talking. The result is a rambling, incoherent message. Stop while you're ahead. You don't have to be wordy. Often, less is more.

Take time to practice responding to questions so you'll be less likely to be caught off guard. Consider video recording yourself so you can listen to your message—the tone and pitch of your voice and the rate of your speech. You can detect if you need to slow down or speak with more variation in your pitch to avoid sounding monotone.

Try to anticipate the main questions you'll be asked and prepare what you'll say. If you do receive a question you didn't expect, buy yourself time by asking the moderator to repeat the question. This will give you a few more seconds to prepare an answer. No matter what the question, plan how you'll weave your message into the answer. That doesn't mean avoiding tough questions. Instead, you're responding to the question in a way that links to your priorities and the message you want to get out to voters.

8. **Ask for feedback on your speeches, debates, and interviews.**

To make it easier to receive honest feedback, ask trusted friends to take notes during campaign events. Also, have them listen to you rehearse your speeches and give you feedback before those events. Phrase your request for feedback in a way that lets the person know you value the information and will use it constructively. State the request by mentioning that you would like to know one thing you did well and one thing that you could improve on for the next time you give a speech or are interviewed.

Sometimes the feedback you receive will not have been solicited and may be phrased in words that are tough to hear. That happened to me on more than a few occasions. If you keep in mind that it's difficult for people to share constructive feedback, it's easier to be appreciative of their efforts, no matter how tactless they might be in the delivery. They're trying to help you get elected, and I believe there's always a kernel of wisdom in all feedback. It's just that sometimes you have to remove the emotion and negativity to be able to identify it. Take time to do that, and always respond to any feedback with "Thank you for sharing that with me. I really appreciate it." This will convey your gratitude and keep the lines of communication open. And say it with a smile because feedback truly is a gift even when it is delivered without the nice packaging of tactful words and phrases.

9. **Always speak in positive terms, even when you are calling for change or criticizing your opponent.**

Use positive language that highlights the change you'll bring. For example, rather than stating, "My opponent has failed to organize a transparent bidding process for county road projects," you could state: "If elected, I'll implement a transparent bidding process for county road projects, something my opponent promised in the last election but has yet to deliver."

It is almost impossible to throw dirt on someone without getting a little on yourself.
—Abigail van Buren, Dear Abby advice columnist

Speaking of your opponent, try to not mention your opponent's name in interviews. Winning an election is all about name recognition, so you don't want to be stating the person's name, further reinforcing it in voters' minds. Instead, say "my opponent." But remember that even when criticizing your opponent, do it in a way that is respectful and use words that call attention to action or inaction and not to personal qualities.

During a debate, refer to your opponent with a courtesy title instead of the office title, especially if your opponent is an incumbent. For example, rather than stating "My proposal differs from Mayor Green's in three important areas," refer to your opponent as "Mrs. Green." This keeps the address formal and courteous without reinforcing the person's incumbency in the minds of voters.

10. **Encourage people to contribute ideas for improving your community by using social media sites such as Facebook and Twitter.**

    Refer to chapter 8 for additional information about using social media.

11. **Visit websites devoted to the governance of counties and towns to get ideas for ways to improve the efficiency and effectiveness of your local government.**

    Businesses and industries are constantly searching for best practices to put to use in their organizations, so it's no surprise that this works well for local government, too. Research what other communities across the country are doing to improve their quality of life, and more than likely you'll find ideas that will be a good fit for your town.

    Where do you start in the search for best practices for local government? Your state most likely has an association of cities and towns that hosts a website with information about best practices and common challenges. These are great sites to obtain ideas on improvements you would like to develop for your community.

    Examples of websites that might be helpful include the National Association of Counties at naco.org and the governing.com website that includes best practices for state and local government.

    If you don't like the way the world is, you change it. You have an obligation to change it. You just do it one step at a time.
    —Marian Wright Edelman, Founder and President of the Children's Defense Fund Founder, first African American woman admitted to the Mississippi State Bar

Questions

1. What are some of the main concerns of people in your community? Which of these concerns are most related to your campaign and most closely linked to what you hope to accomplish when elected?

2. Whom can you ask for honest feedback? How will you state the request so that the person will know you want candid feedback?

3. What are things you can do to prepare for an interview with local media?

Actions

1. Create your elevator speech and practice it by sharing it with your close friends and family. Be sure to ask for their feedback so you can make modifications if necessary.

2. Write your bio specifically for the office you're seeking. Identify the specific skills, experience, and training that qualifies you to hold the office. Make sure these are emphasized in your bio so voters can make the connection

to how your background has prepared you for the responsibilities of the office.

3. Visit websites related to county government to review what other towns have done to improve their communities. Examples include www.naco.org and www.governing.com.

CHAPTER 3

Developing Your
Campaign Strategy

Start your campaign off right by taking the time to commit a campaign strategy to paper. The strategy is your plan for how to run your campaign and win the election. The way you document your strategy is up to you. One way is to treat it as a business plan with a specific mission, objectives, and a timeline. Of course the pressing goal is for you to win the election, but the larger mission is to bring about the change you envision for your community. Just as in a business setting, your mission statement needs to set you apart from your competition.

1. **Determine what is the most important thing that distinguishes you from your opponent.** Don't leave this up to the voters to figure out. It might be that you're the only one running for the office who has experience as a small business owner. Or maybe you're the only one running for office who has been a lifelong resident of the community.

2. **Your main timeline will be the election (and the primary if you are opposed in a partisan race).** But break down the timeline into smaller goals you can track along the way to motivate your team and gauge your progress. Having mini

milestones gives you a reason to celebrate, and it's a good way to keep everyone motivated.

Examples of mini milestones

- percentage of needed funds raised for the campaign
- number of absentee ballots submitted
- a certain number of doors knocked on or neighborhood blocks walked
- number of yard signs posted

3. **Announce your candidacy early, as soon as you make the decision to run and as early as you can in the campaign cycle.**

This may help you avoid competition in the primary since potential candidates might be waiting to see how strong the competition will be before deciding to run. If they see you as a strong candidate, they may be less likely to enter the race. However, if you wait until closer to the filing deadline, and people have already announced their candidacy, it's unlikely they'll drop out of the race.

The benefit of avoiding a contested primary is that it saves you money that you can spend during the general election. But if you do end up having opponents in the primary, there a couple of reasons to view it as a positive. First of all, it makes you get your game together early on. Secondly, it gives you name recognition since people and the press pay more attention to contested races.

Before announcing your campaign publicly, take the time to tell your extended family and trusted friends in advance. You should also consider scheduling a meeting with your employer before you announce it so they won't be taken off guard by the news.

Also, you can assure them that you are committed to keeping your campaign separate from your job. Remember the saying that you don't want to surprise your allies. This includes family, friends, and of course, your employer.

4. **Write down the numbers of votes you'll need to win, and state this as the goal.**

Specifically how many votes will you need to win the election? Visit the county or city's website and search the last election for that office. View the total votes the winner received. Then compare the number of registered voters in that election with the number of registered voters in the current year. This should give you a good idea if the total votes needed will be the same. Write down that number and let your campaign know that this is the goal: *We will win the election by getting 10,250 votes.*

The reason most people never reach their goals is that they don't define them, learn about them, or ever seriously consider them as believable or achievable.
—Dennis Waitley, as quoted in *Life 101*

During my campaign, there was a large increase in the number of newly registered voters because of the presidential election. You can never assume voters in the presidential election, especially those newly registered, will continue down the ballot and vote for candidates in local races. The challenge is to motivate them to not just stop at the top of the ticket. You have to give voters a reason to care about the local races, which is why you have to strategize and plan your race.

5. **Create a campaign countdown to remind you and your family that there is an end in sight to the many days of campaigning.**

   You'll feel like you're running a marathon. And, just like with a marathon, it's good to know there is a finish line. You will make it! Create a visual symbol to represent the countdown. For example, it could be marking off the days on a posted calendar or coloring bricks on a road visual so as the colors appear, you're getting that much closer to the destination. Be creative, and then track the days so you'll approach each day realizing you're that much closer to your goal.

6. **Decide on a reward for you and your family to look forward to as encouragement throughout the campaign season.**

   Throughout the many weekend afternoons and weeknights of events, it will help you to know that the day after the election you'll have something in addition to a victory to replenish your spirits.

   One candidate I worked with planned a week-long fishing trip just after the primary so he could recharge before gearing up for the general election. This helped his energy level before and after the much-deserved time away.

   The reward could be a weekend away or even a day trip to a nearby town or city. The important thing is that it is something you and your family choose at the beginning of the campaign. Be specific in exactly what you will do. Write the event on the specific date on the calendar and also create a flyer with the information, along with a visual image. Put this in a highly visible area in your home so you and your family can see it and be encouraged to work toward the finish line.

Also think of the intangible rewards you will reap as a candidate. When I decided to run, I did what I normally do with important decisions—I listed the personal pros and cons and then weighed them before tallying the score. Some of the positives I listed included learning more about my community and meeting neighborhood and volunteer groups I didn't even know existed before the campaign. I had a much better appreciation of my community and knew more about the strengths and opportunities for growth than before I entered the race.

Another positive I listed was learning how to market my campaign, which can be applied to all types of careers and businesses. Following the campaign, I was surprised by the number of doors that opened because of the visibility of being a candidate. One example was an invitation to co-host a local political TV news segment.

Questions

1. What is a goal you worked to achieve? How did you approach achieving that goal?

    Are there things you did to meet the goal that you can apply to winning the election?

2. Do you think you'll have opposition in the primary? Do you know who will oppose you in the general election?

3. What would you like to do to celebrate your win?

Actions

1. Review data from past elections and the number of newly registered voters to estimate how many votes you'll need to win. Write this number down and share it with your campaign committee.

2. Post your list of pros for running for office in a place where you'll see it often.

3. Write down at least three mini milestones for your campaign and describe how you'll celebrate them with your campaign team.

CHAPTER 4

Building a Strong
Campaign Team

In addition to being a great candidate, you also need to surround yourself with strong and talented people who know what needs to be done and know how to obtain the resources to get them done. That's why choosing your campaign team is one of the most important decisions you'll make as a candidate. Treat it that way rather than merely asking those closest to you in the form of friends and family because you believe they'll feel obligated to say yes. You want people on board who have experience running campaigns and who believe in your candidacy.

Members of your immediate family will likely help you regardless of whether or not they're officially serving on the committee. Expanding the committee beyond family and close friends gives you more backing to recruit volunteers and campaign contributions. Campaign committees vary, but the most basic roles you'll need committee members to serve include:

- manager
- treasurer
- publicity/advertising
- fundraiser

The roles of manager and treasurer are separate positions, but the other functions can be combined. Think of the campaign committee as your board of directors, helping set the vision and strategy of your campaign. You'll need other people to help you implement it.

1. **Ask your local party for help in forming your campaign committee.**

    They'll know the movers and shakers in the community. Also ask your family and circle of friends for recommendations of people to approach. However, also extend your focus to those you know through volunteer work. The most important positions to fill are the campaign manager and the treasurer. Once these positions have been filled, meet with this group to brainstorm the names of other people in the community who share your values and who could provide connections and organizational skills to add strength to your campaign.

2. **When forming your campaign committee, be sure to include a broad spectrum of your community.**

    For example, members could include a teacher, a business owner, a banker, an employee represented by a labor union, and a retiree. Strive to make your campaign committee a culturally diverse group of people who represent your community. Make an inventory of the backgrounds, perspectives, and skills your campaign requires so you can be more strategic in choosing people who round out your team. For example, you might need a person who excels in using social networking tools, as well as someone who has experience in planning fundraising events. If you're running for a city-wide or county-wide office, you'll want people on your committee who represent the different geographical areas of your district.

When asking people to join your committee, take the time to compliment them on the individual strengths they'll bring to your team and ask them the particular tasks and assignments they're most interested in. This lets them know you value their talents. Give all prospective committee members an overview of what their role entails and some of the specific things you'll be asking them to do.

3. **If you know someone whose values you share who is considering running for office in the near future, invite the person to be involved in your campaign.**

Future candidates will be motivated to help and will be engaged since their reasons for being involved are twofold. It's tempting to relegate the duty of recruiting volunteers to someone in your committee, but the best person to do the inviting is you, the candidate. However, if someone on your committee has a solid relationship with an individual you would like to recruit, have that person introduce you or make the first pitch.

If some of the people you ask aren't able to volunteer, don't take it personally. Their situation or schedule might change in the months ahead, or perhaps they'll be able to contribute in another way. Always keep the door open.

4. **Recruit a trusted friend or family member to go with you to events so you will have visible and tangible support.**

This person does not need to be someone on your campaign committee but instead a close friend with whom you're free to share your concerns. They should be someone who knows you well enough to be able to give you candid feedback about how you handled an event. They can observe voters' reaction to you and your message. Also, they can help you if you don't remember names of people you've met. The person can extend her hand and give her name in the greeting, at which time the person should respond in kind, saving you the embarrassment of not remembering the person's name.

However, there's nothing wrong with asking the person's name again. It could be stated as *"It's good to see you again. I remember meeting you last month, but I'm having trouble remembering your name."*

5. **Establish one person you can call to vent your frustrations and share your concerns and fears.**

    This is important because you have to project a positive, upbeat attitude for your campaign team and your volunteers. You will have days when you feel discouraged, but you do not want to let on to your volunteers. You need for them to be upbeat and optimistic, and they'll take their cues from you. For me, this person was a relative who lived miles away from my community, which was ideal.

6. **Always have an agenda for your meetings with your committee and your volunteers.**

    E-mail it several days in advance so attendees will come prepared to participate and take the appropriate action needed. Have copies ready to distribute at the beginning of the meeting. To encourage discussion to stay on track and make the best use of everyone's time, post the agenda so it can serve as a visual reminder as to what needs to be covered in the allotted time. This will give the meeting leader a chance to avoid lengthy interruptions with a reminder of where you are on the agenda.

7. **Ask someone on your committee to take notes at the meetings, especially capturing action items, including what needs to be done, by whom, and by when.**

E-mail the notes soon after the meeting to all committee members, even those who were unable to attend. This keeps everyone in the loop and reminds the team of the campaign's direction and activities. Some candidates have expressed concerns about e-mailing this information, fearing that it could be inadvertently leaked to the competition. But I also heard a campaign field organizer for a congressional candidate argue that the most important thing is following the game plan rather than being concerned it could be shared with others outside the campaign. He always said that if they stuck with the plan and implemented it, the campaign would be successful.

Questions

1. What are the talents and resources your campaign committee needs?

2. Have you already identified key people to serve on your committee? If not, which person or persons could you call to get advice about the people in the community you should invite to be part of your committee?

3. Think back to meetings you've attended that were well run and those that weren't. What were the differences between the two? Are there tactics and tips you can pull from the good example to run your meetings more effectively? Would

you feel comfortable having your campaign manager run some of your meetings if needed?

Actions

1. Finalize your campaign team. Make sure everyone has all committee members' contact information to make it easier to schedule and coordinate meetings and events.

2. Develop your campaign calendar, making sure to note any dates you won't be available due to work or other obligations. See if someone from your campaign committee can attend in your place.

3. Set your first meeting date to get organized and develop the agenda.

CHAPTER 5

Building a Volunteer Base

In addition to a campaign committee, you'll need volunteers to help you get your name out and encourage people to vote. This means knocking on doors, handing out flyers about your candidacy, distributing yard signs, and standing outside the polls on Election Day.

Often, people's time is more precious to them than their money. And with today's busy schedules, people are not looking for activities to fill their day. Knowing these time constraints, you'll need to not be shy about sharing your passion for your campaign. As people see the excitement you have for the changes you want to bring to the community, they'll be more likely to want to contribute time to your campaign. Your volunteers will be the ambassadors of your campaign and need to be updated about decisions and issues impacting it. Pay attention to what they need to do their jobs well and make sure they're aware of how important they are and how much you appreciate their efforts.

A good place to start recruiting volunteers is by asking your campaign committee to ask their friends, neighbors, and families. Every time you're asked to speak to a group, let them know you're looking for volunteers.

1. **Buy a stack of thank-you cards and use them up!**

   If your budget permits, have cards printed with your campaign logo. There are many low-cost options, such as Vista Print and other online printing companies. Just be sure the paper is of good quality and a neutral color to reflect professionalism.

   Show your gratitude for the many ways people will help you along the way. It should be a short, handwritten note that spells out exactly what the person did and how much you appreciate the support for your campaign. Write and mail the card as soon after the favor as possible.

2. **Collect e-mail addresses of volunteers and supporters.**

   You don't want to flood them with e-mails, but at key times this will enable you to spread the word about voting deadlines and events without having to spend a dime (other than the investment of your time).

3. **Invite your volunteers to attend committee meetings.**

   This gives opportunities to volunteers who would like to get more involved. You want to be inclusive in all your campaign events and activities. Go out of your way to involve people by asking for their suggestions and input. Give them advance notice of the schedule of events. And be sure to let them know that whatever time they're able to give is valued and appreciated.

4. **Make a list of tasks or duties that volunteers can do to help you.**

   People are often interested in helping but are not always sure exactly how they can help. You could make a handout titled *The Top 10 Ways to Help Cross the Finish Line.*

5. **Host a cookout for your volunteers a week before the election.**

   This can serve two purposes: 1) to thank them for their hard work; and 2) to rally everyone's spirits to provide momentum for the finish line.

6. **Acknowledge volunteers with award prizes or certificates, such as "Most Miles Walked" or "Post-it Note King."**

Questions

1. What are specific things you can do to engage your volunteers?

2. What information will be helpful to e-mail volunteers and supporters during the campaign season?

3. What are things you can do to recognize volunteers to let them know you appreciate their time and dedication?

Actions

1. Order thank-you cards and be quick to use them.

2. List the tasks volunteers can perform to help your campaign.

3. Plan a cookout or similar event for volunteers a week before the election. Secure the date on your campaign calendar.

CHAPTER 6

Getting Organized

Just as with any project, you're more likely to succeed if you're organized and you know exactly where things are. Campaigns require much paperwork and information gathering, so being well organized is key to being a successful candidate. Preparing for debates and for what's ahead on any given week will be much easier if you make a commitment to stay organized. The time you spend up front will save you hours of aggravation later on.

1. **Designate a space to house your campaign "headquarters."**

   It could be a section of your living room or kitchen or a desk in the family room. Choose a space where the things you'll need to work with are within easy reach. Plus, the space should be free of distractions to enable you to concentrate on the administrative tasks of your campaign, such as answering e-mails and calls, writing thank-you notes, and crafting fundraising letters. You won't need much space since your committee meetings are best held at a public space to allow more room.

2.   **Create a campaign binder.**

Use dividers and plastic sleeves to collect information and to help you check your information at a glance. Examples of organizational tabs include Calendar, Campaign Committee, Fundraising, Issues, Precinct Committee, and Volunteers. Under the Calendar tab, I printed monthly calendar pages from Outlook and wrote the deadlines for campaign finance reports, along with the dates of my fundraisers and those of other local candidates. Even if you work with your files and dates electronically, it's good to have a printout and a quick visual of upcoming events.

3.   **Budget your time.**

Decide how much time you can reasonably devote to your campaign and then budget your time accordingly. Once the primary season is done, there will be events almost every day of the week. If you're balancing your campaign with full-time work and raising a family, you need to be strategic about how to best use your time.

Determine the critical, high-priority things you must do, such as debates, main neighborhood association candidate nights, and fundraising events. Plug these in first and then prioritize the remaining items to see if there are more activities and events than there are available hours in the week, which is very likely.

Set criteria for events you'll attend. Look for events where you have a chance to meet the most voters or have a chance to meet a new group of voters. For my campaign, I looked for opportunities to meet new voters and also chances to listen to voters' concerns on issues. Although I attended parades, had my time been more limited, parades would have been last on my list, but this might be different for other communities. For some events that you can't attend, see if a volunteer or campaign committee member can attend in your place.

4. **Have a calendar of your campaign committee meetings so your team can plan ahead to attend.**

Plan the frequency of meetings and their dates strategically, meeting enough to keep the momentum going but not so frequently that your team feels that they're meeting just to be meeting.

5. **Establish your campaign outfits.**

You'll need a suit for formal events and business casual for informal events such as community festivals and fairs. When the campaign season is in full swing, you'll be so busy that it's best to choose several outfits that will fit the core occasions. Make sure they're in good shape and fit well. Also, select an outfit that will work well for any televised interviews or debates. You'll want to wear solids instead of stripes or a busy pattern since these can appear blurred on television. Wear colors that will complement your appearance and put you in a positive light. If you get these outfits together in advance, you'll have time to try them on and get them altered and dry-cleaned if needed.

Try the outfits on, and ask for feedback from your friends or family. Think about the image you're trying to convey to voters. What specific words do you want voters to use when describing you? Write these down, and share them with your friends or family. Ask them if your overall appearance in the campaign outfits matches those descriptions. Keep working on that until you can say yes. Wear only those things that make you feel confident because how you feel will be conveyed in the way you carry and present yourself. Once you've got them, these outfits, along with your name tag, will become your campaign "uniform."

No matter what event you are attending and how much time you're given to speak, people will have a chance to take in your visual message (your attire and overall image) much more than they will have an opportunity to hear you speak. And even when you're speaking, people are still taking into account your nonverbal communication every bit as much as your verbal message.

I remember one event I attended in which candidates were seated in the first few rows of a large meeting hall. Each candidate was given just three minutes to address the group. With candidates from neighboring counties, the event lasted almost three hours. But, before and after our slated time, the audience definitely had a chance to get a sense of who the candidates were by observing their reactions to other speakers, the way they were dressed, and whether or not they acted like they wanted to be there.

No matter what your outfit, the most important thing to have on is a smile—a genuine one that shows you're enjoying the campaign and meeting the people in your community. People need to see that you truly want the job and will enjoy the work that comes along with it.

Questions

1. How much time per week will you need to dedicate to your campaign?

2. What words do you want voters to use to describe you as a candidate?

3. Does your attire and overall appearance convey those descriptors? If not, what are some things you could do differently to improve your image?

Actions

1. Designate your campaign office or working space, and organize it with the supplies you'll need.

2. Create your campaign binder. Develop sections within it to organize the main functions of your campaign (Advertising/ Marketing, Campaign Committee, Campaign Finance Reports, Fundraising Events, Get-Out-the-Vote Plan, etc.).

3. Determine the main types of events you'll attend for your campaign, and match these event types with specific outfits. Planning your campaign "uniforms" will save you time.

CHAPTER 7

Raising Funds

Just as in the national races, local races have become increasingly costly. It's not uncommon for candidates to spend much more than the salary of the office they're seeking. My campaign for an at-large county seat cost just under $17,000. The position paid $18,688 per year before my local party's 10 percent assessment.

The bulk of your funds will be spent paying for advertising and marketing to get your name, face, and message in front of voters so they'll remember you on Election Day. As an example, more than $3,000 of my campaign went to promotional materials, such as yard signs, T-shirts, buttons, and bumper stickers. The greatest cost was advertising, such as direct mail, newspapers, radio, and billboards. This cost just over $9,600. The more you're able to promote your name through low- or no-cost means, the less money you'll need. That said, you'll still need money to put your campaign in motion.

Candidates often cite raising funds as the most difficult part of campaigning. It's tough to ask people for money, but it's something you must do. Keep in mind why you want to run, the changes you hope to bring to your community, and that a contribution to your campaign is an investment in your community's future. In essence, you're asking people to fund your campaign not for your personal benefit but for the good of the community.

1. **Set your budget and stick to it!**

   There will always be additional items that are costly, so it's best to research what you can afford and then decide how the money will be allotted based on what is practical.

   Since campaign budgets will vary by community and based on the elected office and competition, try to get a good idea of what candidates for that office in your community have spent. Check with your election office to view the financial reports of past candidates. This will illustrate how much money others have spent and how they have spent their campaign funds. After getting this baseline, you and your campaign team can look at how best to reach the voters you're targeting. Some of this will be in paid advertising, which will account for the largest percentage of your campaign costs. Advertising represented approximately 75 percent of my campaign's expenditures.

2. **Check these campaign financial reports from local officeholders' previous campaigns for the list of contributions they received.**

   This will give you insight into the individuals and organizations you might approach to ask for a contribution. Since this will include donations large enough to require reporting, this information could increase your chances of tapping into larger contributions. Armed with this information, you'll be better prepared to decide how high to make your contribution request.

3. **Once you know your budget, write down how many contributions of a specific level you'll need to receive.**

   For example, if you need to raise $15,000, that would equate to …

   15 contributions of $1,000
   30 contributions of $500
   60 contributions of $250
   75 contributions of $200
   150 contributions of $100
   300 contributions of $50
   600 contributions of $25

   Talk with your campaign treasurer and others on your committee to establish targets for your fundraiser. For example, if you make the beginning contribution level $25, you'll need to invite twice as many people as you would if the starting amount is $100 per person.

4. **If your campaign will be affiliated with a political party, check with your local party chair to see if there are any expenses or fees that you will be expected to pay.**

   I was surprised to learn that my county party charged an assessment of 10 percent of what the candidate would receive as a salary for the office if elected. In my case, this was more than $1,500. Money collected from candidates was used to cover the administrative costs of running the party. This fee was due whether or not the candidate won.

If there is a fee, see if it is negotiable. If you have been asked to run and the party has had difficulty fielding a candidate for that particular office, first request that your fee be waived. If the answer is no, ask that the fee be reduced. It doesn't hurt to ask, and if you're successful, you'll have that much more money to invest in advertising and marketing to get your name in front of potential voters. Remember, the worst they can say is no, and even then, they might be willing to reduce or at least delay the date when the payment is due.

Tip: Ask contributors to make checks out to your campaign instead of to the local party, and ask for checks to be mailed directly to your campaign. This allows you to receive the funds more quickly and put them to work for your race. Plus, if you owe an assessment to the party, you'll be able to time your payments to best suit your campaign's needs instead of risking that the party will pressure you to pay your assessment up front by taking it out of your contribution checks that were mailed to their office.

5. **Recruit multiple hosts for your fundraisers.**

   Ask community leaders to serve as honorary hosts of your fundraisers so you can add their name to the invitation, increasing your credibility as a candidate. Plus, you can ask them if they'll share their contacts' mailing information with you so you can expand your network of people to invite. You and your committee will do the work of setting up and hosting the event.

6. **Hold a fundraiser as early as possible in the campaign season.**

   You'll be competing for the total dollars supporters have to invest in several candidates. Since there is a finite amount, you'll want to schedule your fundraiser early. If you're running as a candidate affiliated with a party, check with the local party's headquarters to put your event on the calendar. Often they have a rule that there can only be one fundraiser on any given date. Besides, you'll want to have a date that's clear of scheduling conflicts to increase the chances of people being able to attend your event.

If you're not careful, the cost of holding a fundraiser can result in netting very little in dollars to invest in your campaign. To guard against this, keep your expenses to the bare minimum. First, look for a free or very low-cost venue. Some local bars will provide the space for free as long as you purchase a drink ticket for each guest. Or, you could host the event at a supporter's home or during off hours at their place of business if they're comfortable with this arrangement. Depending upon their type of business, this might not be a problem for them or their customers.

For my fundraiser for the primary, we chose a breakfast event since it was much cheaper than a lunch or dinner option. Depending on your target audience, consider using Facebook and e-mail for paperless invitations to events. Even if you're mailing invitations, you can supplement them with a Facebook invitation. Just be careful about Facebook RSVPs for your food and beverage count since the etiquette is more relaxed, making RSVPs not as reliable.

7. **Send invitations to your fundraisers to candidates of the same political party.**

If you're not in a partisan race, send invitations to candidates for other offices regardless of their political party. Personalize the invitation to let them know you would like them to be your guest at the event so they know they aren't expected to give you a contribution.

That will give them a chance to meet more potential new contacts in addition to increasing the number of people attending your event. Also, attendees will have an opportunity to meet potential officeholders and pose their questions and concerns. It's a benefit to everyone, and the candidates may return the favor and invite you to their fundraisers free of charge, giving you a chance to gain visibility with more voters and potential supporters.

8. **Recruit college students to help you at the event.**

They can staff the registration table and greet newcomers as they arrive. It gives them a chance to attend events for free and meet people in the process.

9. **Plan a fundraising event with a group of candidates if appropriate and center it around a sport or hobby.**

In my community, one common fundraising vehicle is a golf outing where funds are raised in several ways. Sponsorships are sold for each hole, and there are registration fees for players.

During my campaign, the female candidates in our political party combined our efforts and hosted a card party, which is a popular recreational fundraising activity in our community. We sold tickets and collected donated items from individuals and businesses for raffles and others game prizes. In addition to receiving money for all four women's campaigns, we also met new voters and volunteers at the event. This wasn't as lucrative as sporting events, so be sure to estimate the time involved and the average amount of total funds to expect for a particular fundraiser. One fundraiser that took off in our community was a poker card tournament. However, depending upon your campaign platform and community makeup, this may or may not be appropriate. That's why it is so important to know your community and take this knowledge into account when planning your fundraising events.

10. **Don't make the mistake I did and offer a discounted contribution for "couples" attending your fundraising event.**

One person let me know that although she would still write me a check, she wouldn't be attending because she was offended by the implied affront to single people. If you opt to give a discount, phrase it as "$50 per ticket or $75 for you and a friend."

11. **Have name tags at the sign-in table at all your campaign events.**

These don't need to be preprinted. Just be sure to have sticker-type name tags and a bold permanent marker so people can write their own as they arrive. This will help you work on remembering people's names and will make it easier for people to get to know each other and enjoy the event.

12. **Provide visuals at your fundraising events.**

One fundraising event I attended featured a slideshow of photos of the candidate at past community and political events. The slides transitioned on a large television screen and kept repeating. It was visible in the background, but since it was just a visual without sound, it wasn't distracting yet was still noticeable and effective. The more you can include photos of contributors and volunteers who will be at your event the better. If they've been photographed with you helping at various events in the past several years, be sure to include these. They'll enjoy receiving the credit, and it will make your slideshow more interesting.

13. **Be sure to take the stage at some point during your fundraiser.**

Midway through the event, get everyone's attention and talk briefly about why you're running and how much you appreciate their help. But first thank all your hosts (calling on them individually) and volunteers at the event. It's also a nice courtesy to introduce the officeholders and other candidates who are there. Have a person at the registration table keep a list of officeholders as they sign in for the event so you'll be sure not to miss anyone.

14. **Give campaign T-shirts as door prizes at your fundraising events.**

Also, have campaign buttons or stickers at the registration table and encourage people to take them.

15. **Make sure to mail handwritten thank-you cards within a couple of days after your fundraiser.**

Any thank-you note, whether it's an e-mail or phone call, will do, but a handwritten one is best. To make it easier to send a handwritten note, you can print the same short message on your campaign letterhead and then add a handwritten personal note at the bottom. Be sure to use mail merge to address the letter to the person rather than a generic greeting. The following is sample wording for a thank-you note to contributors.

Dear Steve,

Thank you so much for your $250 contribution to my campaign for an at-large seat on the Vanderburgh County Council. And thank you for your encouragement and for spreading the word to your neighbors, family, and friends who live in the county.

If elected I will do my best to serve the residents of our county by working for

- Responsible, responsive, and transparent government of the people;
- Economic, workforce, job, and general community development; and
- Quality of life amenities that will keep and attract young people.

With warmest regards,

Tammy

Tammy R. Barnett
Candidate for Vanderburgh County Council At-Large

16. **Know your state's reporting requirements for political campaign contributions.**

    Contact your county or city's election clerk to obtain this information and answers to your questions. Distribute this information to your campaign committee to make sure everyone involved understands the requirements.

Never allow a person to tell you no who doesn't have the power to say yes.
—Eleanor Roosevelt

17. **Call and write local political and trade organizations to ask for their support and for a contribution.**

   Many have a formalized process, and they will ask candidates to complete a form and then be interviewed by their leadership team or political action committee. Even if they do not have a formalized process, they might have a budget for political contributions. If you don't ask, you can be sure you will not receive any funds. Contact them as early as possible.

Questions

1. Think about fundraising events you have attended.

   What did you like about the event?

   What were things you would do differently?

   What ideas can you use as you plan your fundraisers?

2. What are locations in your community that would be good for your fundraising events?

3. Whom could you ask to serve as honorary hosts of your fundraising events?

Actions

1. Obtain a copy of your state's campaign finance laws. Read them in their entirety and also ask your treasurer and your campaign committee to read them. Seek help from the city or county clerk or election board for answers to any questions you or your campaign committee have.

2. Determine your campaign budget and commit it to paper.

3. Make a list of associations and organizations in your community that you plan to approach for contributions to your campaign.

CHAPTER 8

Getting Your Name Out

You might be the most qualified person for the office, with the best experience and skills, but if voters don't know your name or forget it before the election, you don't stand a chance of winning. That's why getting your name and image before voters and communicating a message that sticks with them is the most important part of your campaign. This is all the more challenging if you're running the same year as the presidential election since all attention will be focused at the top of the ticket.

1. **If you are running against an incumbent, you must give voters a reason to desire a change.**

    Remember that when you're calling for change, be sure to present it in a positive light. This is critical because people want to feel inspired and hopeful about the future. Avoid talking in terms of doom and gloom.

    If you are the incumbent running against a challenger, present yourself as someone who gets things done. Stress all the accomplishments made during your time in office, plus additional improvements that are in progress and will continue when you are re-elected.

2. **Have a professional headshot photo taken.**

This is one of the first things you should do, well before announcing your candidacy. This headshot will be used many times and in many ways throughout your campaign. Wear a suit to show your professionalism and use accessories such as a tie or scarf to add a splash of color. Be sure to smile to convey friendliness and approachability. Voters need to see you as a likeable person in order to want to give you their vote.

Be sure to ask the photographer for the photo file in addition to the prints so you can upload it to your website and Facebook page. You can send the photo file with the press release announcing your candidacy to the media. More than likely, if the photo is of good quality, they'll run it with the article if space permits.

3. **Invest in professionally engraved name tags for yourself and your campaign committee and ask them to wear them to campaign events.**

These should be a larger font that is simple to read and should be simply stated: *Jan Smith for County Council*. A white background makes it easier for the lettering to stand out and be seen. Plan to wear your name tag *everywhere*, with church and your place of employment being two of the few exceptions.

Place your name tag on your right side because you use your right hand to extend a handshake. This means the person will be looking toward your right side during the handshake and will be more likely to focus on your name. This increases the chance of people remembering your name when they see it on the ballot.

4. **Have campaign buttons printed and ask volunteers to wear them to campaign and community events to help you spread the word.**

Stickers are okay, too, although they don't last. However, because they take little effort to put on, more people will be willing to take one and put it on at events. They might keep the sticker on their jackets as they stop at the grocery store or gas station on the way home from your event. Examples of community events include National Night Out, county and 4-H fairs, and church socials.

5. **Develop and print campaign T-shirts for your volunteers who will stand at the polls.**

Choose a bright color with clear and easy-to-read lettering so they are not only noticeable but also legible from a distance. Also check the price of printing on the back of the shirt so you can double the opportunity for people to see the message.

6. **Yard signs are a much better investment than bumper stickers.**

Although yard signs are more expensive than bumper stickers, they're a better value because more people are willing to take and display them than bumper stickers. It's fairly easy to display a yard sign, while a bumper sticker takes more effort to affix and then remove once the election is over. Some people don't like to use bumper stickers because of the sticky residue and marks they leave on their automobiles. If you do decide to have both, consider having more yard signs than bumper stickers.

Choose a simple design that's easy to read. If you can include your photo in the design, it can add to the effectiveness. You'll want a clear font style that's easy to read as people drive by. It should be strong on the visuals and contain as few words as possible. For example, rather than spelling out the full name of the office, you might be able to make it concise. My signs said "Elect Barnett for County Council." Since the only council seats on the ballot for that election were at-large seats, I didn't need to spell out "at-large." Include an action verb such as *vote* or *elect*.

Visit websites of companies that print campaign material to get ideas of designs and wording. Word of caution: check with your political party headquarters in your community to see if there are written or unwritten rules about printing these. It might be that your business community will notice if you choose to keep your money in the community by having your signs printed by a local company. In my community, candidates running on the Democratic ticket were strongly urged to have all materials (yard signs, T-shirts, and especially fundraising invitations) produced at a union print shop. Union representatives wanted to see the union logo on materials of candidates to whom they gave their financial support.

7. **Consider using billboards to gain name recognition.**

Depending upon your community, if you can select a billboard in a key area, it can be very effective in attracting attention. Consider having your photo on the billboard. Keep it simple, with your name and the office you are seeking. Mine had a black and white headshot with the words *Barnett *Vote* County Council* in three lines. Remember that drivers have only a few seconds to take in your message, so you'll want it to have maximum visual impact.

58

8. **Publicize your filing date in advance to increase your chances of having an audience of supporters.**

    Send a press release to local media (newspaper, radio, and television stations). If it's a slower news day with little to cover, news editors may need content to fill space or airtime.

9. **Create an e-mail address exclusively for your campaign**.

    Having this separate e-mail account will ensure requests for information and volunteers' inquiries don't get lost or hidden in your regular e-mail account. It will help you compartmentalize your messages. Also, it will help you to avoid using a work e-mail address for your campaign, something you definitely do not want to do. Make sure the address is professional and appropriate. For example, Larry4Sherriff is easy to remember and is tailored for the account's purpose.

10. **Volunteer to speak at meetings throughout your community.**

    The more diverse the groups are the better since it will help you spread your message. Potential places to speak include club meetings (Rotary Club, Lion's Club, Optimist Club, Jaycees, etc.), neighborhood association meetings, community colleges, retirement communities, etc. Even if these organizations do not allow candidates to speak, by calling them to inquire about these opportunities, you'll at least be on their radar.

11. **List all your connections to help you better visualize the network you have that you can tap into.**

    On the first run through, you might have a hundred-plus people. Put the list aside and revisit it the next day. Think about all the activities and organizations you're involved in, and soon your list will easily triple. Do you belong to the Parent-Teacher Organization or volunteer at the Red Cross? Are you a member of the Rotary Club or the League of Women Voters?

Don't stop with your connections. Think of the networks the members of your family belong to. Does your daughter belong to the 4-H? Does your spouse play in a tennis league? All these organizations' members share at least some of your and your family's interests and passions, so this is an excellent place to start.

List the organizations you belong to on your campaign material. This will help potential voters in those organizations make the connection with you as a candidate and will increase the likelihood that they'll recognize your name on the ballot. Remember, many voters are so concerned about the national races that they pay little attention to local campaigns. Therefore, you'll need to work extra hard for voters to remember your name and the office you are seeking.

12. **Conduct an e-mail campaign to give you a low-cost way to connect with voters.**

Use e-mails to remind people of upcoming important dates, such as the deadline for applying to vote by absentee ballot. Other information to share could include candidate debates or community forums. You don't want to inundate people's e-mails, so be judicious about the use of e-mails and make sure the content provides information they'll find helpful. Also, make sure you place e-mail addresses in the BC (blind copy) field to protect your supporters' privacy.

13. **Ask a respected politician or community leader who knows you and your ability to perform the duties of the job to provide a statement about you to be included in your campaign materials.**

    This will serve as an endorsement and will give you credibility. You could call the person and make your request and then, depending upon your relationship with the person, offer to send several quotes they can choose from or use as a start.

14. **Create a Facebook page specifically for your campaign.**

    Use it and other social media tools, such as Twitter and YouTube, to reach as many people as possible with no other investment but your time. It will make it easier for you to send announcements, as well as invitations for fundraisers and canvassing events.

15. **Create a website.**

    It doesn't have to be sophisticated. It should be used as a way to educate voters about your background and why you are qualified to hold the office you are seeking. It should give visitors a way to give you feedback and sign up to volunteer with your campaign. At a minimum, it should include a page with your photo and a bio containing your experience and skills relevant to your qualifications for the office. It should include a Contact Us page so visitors know how to get in touch with your campaign to ask about your position on issues or how to volunteer for your campaign. You can also include a link for contributions.

    Younger voters will expect your campaign to have a website. It shows you're up to date with communication technology and gives volunteers an easy way to check on campaign events.

16. **Create a page for your campaign on national websites related to your political party or political beliefs.**

    For example, the Democracy for America (DFA) website provides a place for candidates of local races across the country to create a page about their campaign. You can upload photos, include a bio about your background, and also announce events. This is another way to connect with voters in your area who might be searching for candidates they can support based on shared political views.

17. **Find out whether or not the local newspaper endorses candidates.**

    If they do, research the process so you can be prepared whether it's an interview or completing a questionnaire or both. Even if the paper does not endorse candidates, call the editor to set up a meeting to introduce yourself. It will be beneficial to meet with the editor and possibly the editorial board face-to-face. You should share with them why you're running for office and the goals you'll work to achieve for your community. Even if they don't endorse candidates, they are voters, and if you make a good impression on them, you'll earn their vote and possibly the votes of others in their circle of influence.

18. **Contact professional associations, trade organizations, and labor unions to seek their support.**

    Depending on your platform and the issues you support, you might be in alignment with various business or trade organizations or labor unions. Contact these organizations and ask whether or not they endorse candidates, and if so, what the process is to secure their endorsement. Then, see what connections you or your supporters might have with members in the organization so they can put in a good word for you.

If you don't receive the endorsement, give it a positive spin by emphasizing that as a candidate without ties to special interests, you will be an independent voice for voters.

19. **Write letters to the editor stating your position or support of specific local issues or events that are important to you and voters.**

Your letter could be a note of thanks to an agency or organization that has completed an important milestone or community initiative. For example, if the parks department has completed a new walking path, you could write a letter commending the accomplishment. Within the letter, you could mention how this achievement will positively impact the community. Having your letters published in the newspaper gives you free publicity.

20. **Ask your supporters to write letters to the editor stating why you are a good candidate.**

These letters should mention specific examples of things you have done for the community or reasons you would be a good choice for the office. Letters that include these specifics are more sincere and thus more persuasive to readers.

21. **Host a postcard-writing party.**

Invite friends, family, and supporters to bring a list of addresses for their neighbors, family, coworkers, and friends. Have the postcards printed with your name and the office you're seeking at the top of the card. Volunteers will then include a personal note asking their contacts to vote for you.

Serve plenty of snacks and refreshments so it will be fun. The women's caucus in my community did something similar for the women running for local office. It gave us a chance to support the candidates in a tangible way. Later, some members heard from friends and neighbors that they appreciated the postcard and that it resulted in their vote.

The postcard is a good format since it's cheaper to mail and catches the recipient's attention without them having to take the time to open an envelope. Plus, letter carriers across the city will see your message as well, possibly persuading them to vote for you.

Resource: To find zip codes, visit the US Postal Service website. Type in the address to receive the zip code.

22. **Proofread all campaign materials (e-mails, thank-you letters, candidate questionnaires, etc.) carefully.**

Then ask several people to proofread your materials. It's a good idea to ask someone to review your material who is not involved with your campaign but who has a good sense of the community. They will be more likely to pick up on red flag words or terms that might have different meanings for the various constituent groups in your community.

For example, I included the term "corrective actions" and then changed this to "solutions" after discovering that corrective action meant disciplinary action in some of the manufacturing companies in the community.

23. **If your fitness routine includes walking around your neighborhood, always be sure to wear your campaign T-shirt.**

    The more people see you and your name, the more likely they'll be to remember it when they vote. Use your walks as an opportunity to smile and say hello to your neighbors.

24. **If you have a good relationship with a recognized community leader (a respected teacher or principal, a business owner, a coach), ask that person to write a letter to their friends and associates asking them to vote for you.**

    They can list the reasons why you will be good for the office. If people receiving the letter have not heard much about your campaign, this will make them more likely to connect with your name in the future. Their respect for the person writing the letter will make them more receptive to the message and thus more likely to vote for you.

Questions

1. What are the top three ideas mentioned in this section that you could implement relatively quickly?

2. Which organizations and groups do you belong to that could help you increase your visibility with potential voters?

Actions

1. Order your name tag.

2. Schedule your appointment for your campaign photo.

3. List the names of people in your community that you personally know. Try to list at least 250 names. Return to it the next day and see how many additional names you can add. Show the list to your family to see if they know more names to add.

4. Using the list of names, start building your e-mail list for your campaign.

CHAPTER 9

Connecting with Voters

For most voters, choosing which person they'll vote for is more than just an exercise in logic where they read candidates' information in a voter guide and then select the person based on those qualifications. Instead they want to get a sense of the candidate's personality. How likable or approachable is that person? Would this be a person they could feel comfortable having a conversation with over coffee? It can feel like elections in high school where the person winning wasn't necessarily the most qualified but was definitely the most popular. That's why finding ways to connect with voters on a personal level is so important. They want to know if you have things in common with them. Do you share their values and concerns? Will you be a person they'll feel comfortable approaching?

1. **Get involved in a community event in which your campaign can provide a service.**

   For example, your campaign could volunteer to participate in a cleanup day in the park or some other community-organized event.

   The first step is to review the community events occurring during the timeframe of the campaign. Choose the ones that are a good fit for voters you want to reach, and then contact the event organizer to see if there is a service your campaign can provide. For example, if one of your goals as a candidate is to promote beautification and upkeep of the parks and recreational areas, your campaign could volunteer to participate as a team in a cleanup day in the park. One candidate chose to host a water stop at a half-marathon run. Volunteers were given campaign T-shirts so runners would make a connection with the campaign.

2. **Use people's names when you greet them.**

If you're not good at remembering people's names, be more intentional, concentrating on their names as they're introducing themselves.

As a candidate, you'll work to remember as many names as you can, while you've got to assume voters need lots of reinforcement and repetition to remember your name. Just because you've met them at a forum or fair doesn't mean they'll remember your name at election time. That's why it's important to do all you can to get your name in front of voters. It's all about name recognition, which is why those already in the office you're seeking begin with a distinct advantage.

3. **Ask for their vote.**

Every time you are invited to speak during the campaign, always include a statement asking people for their support and for their vote. People want you to ask for their vote.

For example, at the end of your talk, you could state: "I've really enjoyed meeting with your association and learning more about the work you do for our community and the issues important to making that possible. In closing, I would appreciate your support and your vote so I can serve you on the school board. Thank you."

4. **Attend the fairs, festivals, and neighborhood social events where you can meet and visit with people one-on-one.**

As your calendar becomes full and there are events that conflict, be strategic about which activities you attend. For example, some county or regional parades where the attendees are from outside your voting area might not be worth the time. Parades where you're surrounded by other candidates and don't get a chance to shake hands with voters and make a connection may not be an effective use of your time.

5. **Identify a local organization whose cause and mission is aligned with your goals as a candidate.**

For example, if you want to encourage recycling as part of your campaign, meet with a recycling group in the community to share your mission and passion. You can find out ideas they have for how a person in the office you're seeking can make an impact. Or if part of your campaign mission is to create a more fitness-friendly community, you could contact a walking or cycling club and ask if you could attend their next meeting to introduce yourself and listen to their concerns.

6. **Visit local universities and community colleges to meet with their student political and community groups.**

While you're there, ask the students if they are registered to vote. Encourage them to become involved in your campaign to learn more about the process and to meet employers and leaders in the community.

7. **Be sure to walk your own neighborhood and introduce yourself to your neighbors.**

   Knocking on doors and meeting people face-to-face is one of the most effective ways to connect with voters. Don't assume that just because you're neighbors they're aware of your campaign. They might not realize that the Bob Smith running for the school board is the same Bob Smith that lives in the house on the corner.

8. **If your budget permits, have your brochure printed as a door hanger.**

   That way, when you're walking neighborhoods, you'll be able to leave information about your campaign if no one is home to answer the door. Have a pen with you so you can sign the door hanger with a note, such as "Sorry I missed you."

9. **Ask supporters in different neighborhoods to host a meet-and-greet gathering to give you a chance to meet the neighbors and connect with them in a more informal and relaxed setting.**

   This would work well as a backyard cookout or something as simple as coffee and cookies. It's completely up to them. Give them a sample flyer and offer to make copies so they can give it to their neighbors at least a week or two in advance.

10. **Don't be afraid of questions you can't answer.**

    Offer to take people's contact information so you can get back to them with an answer. Then, make sure to follow up! They will be pleasantly surprised. Take a legal pad or notepad with you wherever you go to make sure you capture those questions or issues that require follow-up.

Always do right. This will gratify some people and astonish the rest.
—Mark Twain

Questions

1. Think of local officeholders you have supported and voted for.

   What was it about those candidates that made you decide to support them?

2. What are your areas of expertise related to the office you're seeking?

   What are the areas you'll need help with?

   Who can help you develop strength in those areas?

Actions

1. Identify at least one community event in which your campaign can volunteer to participate.

2. Make a list of the fairs and festivals in your community and put them on your campaign calendar.

3. Choose a local organization whose cause and mission is aligned with your campaign. Schedule a meeting with the organization's leaders to introduce yourself and your campaign.

CHAPTER 10

Getting Out the Vote

No matter how much money you raise, how many volunteers you have, or how good your message is, if you're not able to get enough voters to the polls, you won't win. It's just that simple. That's why the most important thing to concentrate on is Getting Out the Vote. This is called GOTV in campaign lingo. Always keep this in mind, and make sure the majority of your campaign committee's strategy sessions stay focused on this goal—identifying voters who are likely to support you and motivating them to go to the polls and vote for you. This is easier in a general election when other races are on the ballot. However, if you're opposed in the primary, it can be especially challenging to encourage voters to go to the polls, especially if the majority of races in your community are unopposed in the primary.

Because getting out the vote is the most crucial aspect of a political campaign, much has been researched and written about how to get voters to the polls. According to a 2004 book titled *Get Out the Vote! How to Increase Voter Turnout,*[1] by Donald P. Green and Alan S. Gerber, the best way to increase voter turnout is to have direct contact with voters. It's the old-fashioned method of walking down neighborhood streets and meeting voters and talking with

---

[1]   D. P. Green & A. S., *Get Out the Vote! How to Increase Voter Turnout* (Washington, DC: Brookings Institution Press, 2004).

them one-on-one. This continues to be the best way to reach voters and motivate them to take the time to vote. Nothing beats the personal touch. Their second edition published in 2008 reinforces this approach. They refer to a Kansas State Board of Education election and the finding that a more personal connection with voters was usually more effective than an impersonal connection.[2] Because door-to-door contact with voters gives you a chance to make a personal connection, it's a great method for reaching voters.

A political leader in my community shared her inspirational story of knocking on as many doors as possible, even in precincts that historically voted for the other party. She believed there was always an opportunity to win someone's trust and vote if she could meet them one-on-one. She said that many people in areas where the demographics and political slant would seem the last place for her to campaign were surprised and pleased that she took the time to reach out to them. She didn't take a "no" for granted. She continually encourages candidates to pound the pavement and get out there and introduce themselves and ask people for their vote.

1. **If you are running in a seat to represent an entire county or city where it isn't feasible to canvass all the neighborhoods, determine the demographics of voters who would likely support you to decide which areas and neighborhoods to target.**

   If you are running as part of a political party, a natural choice would be to select neighborhoods that have a larger percentage of people registered as supporters of your political party affiliation. To find out the breakdown of these neighborhoods (called precincts), check with the county or city clerk or your local government's website to look at past voting records broken down by precinct. Then, determine how many precincts you

---

[2]   D. P. Green & A. S., *Get Out the Vote! How to Increase Voter Turnout,* Second Edition (Washington, DC: Brookings Institution Press, 2008).

can realistically cover, and based on that, you can choose the top precincts. For my race, there were more than ninety-five precincts, and we targeted the top twenty precincts to walk and also the top 10 to man with volunteers at the polling places on Election Day.

2. **Obtain voter registration forms and always have copies with you to give to people you meet at forums and events who haven't yet registered to vote.**

   In fact, always ask people you meet if they are registered to vote, and if they say no, ask them if they would like to register. You can have them complete the form on the spot, and then you can return it to the election office or fax it there.

   Schedule a meeting with the election official in your community and ask the person to review the rules and procedures for completing an absentee ballot or voter registration form. You'll want to make sure the forms you turn in are completed correctly to avoid having the application delayed or rejected.

3. **Be sure to ask your supporters and volunteers if they are registered to vote.**

   You'll be surprised how many people either have never registered to vote or did not update their voter registration when they moved.

4. **Remind volunteers and supporters to ask their friends, neighbors, and families to vote for you.**

   Often, voters are so inundated with advertisements for national and state campaigns that they aren't aware of some of the local races and will enter the polls without knowing any of the candidates' names. They appreciate information from their personal contacts. If they don't know anything about any of the candidates, they might find themselves voting solely on party affiliation or on perceptions based on candidates' names. Specifically ask volunteers to share information about your candidacy with their friends and family and to ask them to consider voting for you. The more people they contact, the more your vote total will climb.

Several community leaders, friends, and families volunteered to e-mail their contacts to encourage them to vote for me. The following is an example of the e-mail my brother sent along with my bio file before the primary:

Dear Friend,

I'm pleased and proud to share with you that my sister and good friend, Tammy Barnett, is running on the Democratic ticket for County Council at Large.

I feel that our county would be very fortunate to have her as a County Council member. Tammy is extremely focused and talented, and she has a strong work ethic.

If you are able, please vote for her in the primary on Tuesday, May 6th. I have attached her biography, so you can learn about her accomplishments and see that she is well qualified to serve on the County Council. If you have any questions, please email them to me, or call me.

Respectfully,

As the next example illustrates, the e-mail/letter can be brief.

I'm pleased and proud to share that my friend Tammy Barnett is running on the Democratic ticket for the County Council at Large seat. If you get the chance to vote for her, please do.

Nan

5. **Introduce yourself to the precinct committee people in your community.**

   Precinct committee people are the ones who help run the polls on Election Day by serving at their neighborhood's voting precincts. They are usually well connected to their neighbors and are a good source of information so that you know what to expect when you walk the neighborhoods to introduce yourself to voters. Although they're the backbone of a political party, they often don't get the respect and recognition they deserve. They are the people performing the behind-the-scenes work that doesn't get much attention unless it doesn't get done.

   Their contact information can be obtained from the local political party offices. Write a short letter to the precinct committee members introducing who you are and stating your qualifications and how you bring value to the community. Include your contact information and invite them to call you to discuss their ideas and concerns. Your letter will show that you respect their position and influence and the important role they play in getting voters to the polls.

6. **Recruit volunteers to stand at the polls on Election Day.**

   Recruit them early to ensure you'll have ample coverage for the key polling places you've identified.

High school students can make good volunteers at the polls. It's a perk for them because most school districts will excuse their absence, provided students have your campaign or local party office sign a form stating what their duties will be for that day. Check with your local election office to confirm the rules for high school students working at the polls. Then, begin with a relative or neighbor that you know who attends the school. That person can help you recruit responsible, confident students to greet voters and ask for their vote.

7. **Provide your volunteers with specific written instructions about what to do on Election Day.**

It should be a one-page sheet that states their purpose, a sample greeting for voters, and a reminder of the laws in your area that dictate conduct at the polls. Also include a cell number they should call if questions or concerns arise during the day.

I kept my instructions to a simple bulleted list.

Instructions for Election Day Volunteers

- Please wear your Elect Barnett t-shirt and campaign button.
- Please call Greg at 449-XXXX if there is no Barnett sign at
- the polling place.
- Stand in front of the building so you can greet voters as they head to the polls.
- Greet volunteers and say that you hope that they will vote for Tammy Barnett for County Council.
- Thank them for voting as they leave.
- Smile!

If you have any questions or need anything, please call 449-XXXX.

Place the instruction sheet in a bag that includes a few snacks and other items that will help make their time at the polls more enjoyable. You can also use this as a way to show your appreciation for their time and efforts. I stapled the instruction sheet to a treat bag that contained gum, hard candy, and baked goods.

8. **Remind your volunteers who will be working on Election Day to vote by absentee ballot.**

They will be busy that day visiting polling places and may not have time to get to their own polling place in time to vote. That's why it's a good idea for you and your volunteers to vote by absentee beforehand. Visit your county clerk's office or website to obtain an application for an absentee ballot and to review the rules for voting by absentee in your state.

Questions

1. What are the demographics of the voters who would likely support you? (For example, are they small business owners or union members?)

2. How many precincts will you man with volunteers on Election Day?

3. How many precincts will you have volunteers present in on Election Day?

Actions

1. Visit the election office in your community to find out the proper procedure for registering voters and completing applications for absentee ballots.

2. Determine the number of volunteers you'll need to be present at the polls on Election Day.

3. Write an instruction sheet for your volunteers who'll be at the polls.

CHAPTER 11

Challenges Women
Candidates Face

After finishing the tips in this book and asking friends who were involved in local political campaigns to review it, they pointed out that something was missing—a section speaking directly to female candidates ... not because men don't need the same support and resources but because, from our personal experiences, women face unique challenges since historically they have not been part of political circles. These have been comprised mainly of men. While this topic could easily fill the pages of another book, this section reviews the three main challenges that can impact your ability to win and includes tips for overcoming them.

First Challenge: The tendency to wait for an invitation to run for office

Maybe it's the cultural messages young women receive during their teenage years when they're discouraged from asking someone on a date or they avoid voting for themselves in school elections. They're told to wait until they're called, to not look too assertive, to be patient and see what comes to them rather than seeking out what they want. There are strong messages about not being perceived as aggressive or forward when it comes to academics and dating. With these messages, it's easy to understand why some women are tempted to wait until they're asked to enter a political race. This isn't good for any candidate, but especially not for women because the political power brokers, though not consciously keeping women out of politics, will think first of those who are better connected and visible in their own circles, and most often, these are other men.

Women interested in running for office must resist the urge to wait until they're asked to run, because if they wait, they may find themselves invited to enter races merely to fill the ticket. Those races are often last minute and largely viewed as unwinnable. Women may be told that the race will at least give them name recognition and provide them a chance to learn the ropes. Don't buy it! Choose the race that is right for you, and then—and only then—run. And run to win!

Second Challenge: Not thinking big enough when raising funds for the campaign

Women may feel uncomfortable asking for money period, no matter what the sum. Therefore, they are tempted to set the suggested donation levels lower so they won't offend anyone. But if you don't ask for higher levels as early as possible in the election cycle, you'll receive the leftovers. I saw this in my community; male candidates had fewer fundraising events that took less time but garnered more dollars for the time spent. For example, a popular fundraiser in my community is a golf scramble with one of the lower contribution levels set at one hundred dollars. Fundraisers for female candidates (such as card parties) brought in just as many people but relied on many small donations since donation levels began low—for example, with a five-dollar ticket to the event, with the hope people would spend more once they got in the door. This involved even more work and additional time spent asking for donated baked items and services and products that were part of a raffle ticket.

Realize your worth and ask for the top dollar that other candidates are seeking. You'll need it, and by thinking bigger and asking for more, you're much more likely to get the funds you'll need to run a successful race.

Third Challenge: A reluctance to ask for help

Seek out women in your community who have run for office. More than likely, they'll gladly share what they've learned with you. Women who have been through the process know the challenges women face and can steer you in the right direction, helping you tap resources or avoid pitfalls that they encountered.

I noticed that when men volunteered, they made the effort to get credit for what they did. Often, they would specifically state that they were happy to do the favor for you because they might need help from you in the future. I appreciated their honesty and admired how they actively sought to build resources and support for their campaigns. Women are quick to help but often feel awkward about using that as an opportunity to call in those favors when they need them. Speak up for yourself!

Words of Advice

A number of female officeholders and candidates offered the following tips to women running for office. The first is from Indiana Lt. Governor Sue Ellspermann:

Candidates are often coached to run a "contrast campaign," that is, expose the key differences between you and your opponent and "go after" him/her on those areas of difference. That most often leads to eventual "mudslinging" as the back and forth gets more heated. Framing your opponent as the "villain" makes for exciting marketing pieces and headlines.

However, if we ask constituents what they like least about politics, they often say the "mudslinging" and ugly commercials they are forced to endure during campaign years: grainy and distorted pictures, quotes taken out of context, etc. Often these ads take a small thread of reality and distort it into a conspiracy.

As one who spent her life facilitating problem solving teams and building consensus, I made a commitment before I ran to conduct a high integrity campaign with no mudslinging. Zero. That sounds good, but then how can you win?

First, I asked one of my very good friends and strategic marketer, Tonya Brothers-Bridge, to be my campaign manager. Neither of us had ever run a campaign. However, I knew who I was, had a strong career, and a reason for running. She knew how to brand.

Thus, comes the 1-2-3 Method:

1. Tell them who you are.
2. Tell them what you've done.
3. Tell them what you plan to do.

At the end of the day, I believe people want to vote for the best person. I think they want to know who you are, what you stand for and what you aspire to do. I believe they would rather vote for someone, than against someone. I believe Americans still believe our political system can work. However, I believe campaign politics as they are allowed to play out make that very difficult.

We branded me as a problem solver … in which I hold a PhD. We shared my story working with hundreds of organizations and groups in my district, state, and nationally. We developed three main focuses for me: economic development, education, and sanctity of life … all congruent with efforts in which I had been engaged. My story was that of growing up in a small town, one of six children, and becoming a female engineer, entrepreneur, academic, and mother. I had experienced divorce, been a single mother, and now have a beautiful blended family of four young adult daughters.

We started the campaign with a series of Listening Sessions in each community to understand their challenges and aspirations. This helped inform our focus areas. On the campaign trail, I rarely mentioned my opponent's name and didn't criticize his positions, but rather described my positions.

Some of my party's leaders were less than excited with my approach. I believe they felt it "soft" and naïve. In fact, campaign finance groups tried to be helpful by crafting "contrast pieces," which they assured us via polling would give an advantage. We turned them all away. There would be no negative campaigning, win or lose, one of our Ten Commandments of the Campaign.

Upon encouragement by local media, I crafted a Political Civility Agreement which my opponent edited and then we signed at our debate. Neither of our parties was enthused with this approach. I was still polling as a ten-point underdog. Again, some party leaders thought I couldn't win this way.

The 1-2-3 approach isn't easy or cheap. You have to do all the basics well: door-to-door, fundraising, phone banks, parades, and events. From palm cards to yard signs and mail pieces, the message has to brand and reinforce the candidate. We used social media, television ads, billboards, mobile advertising, and personal letters. It cost us 50 percent more than originally budgeted. We also did not respond to negative editorials which were published against me. We focused on who I was, what I had done and what I would do if elected. Period.

We won the race 52–48 in an underdog district. Voters thanked me on Election Day for the race we ran … many who likely did not vote for me. It was the upset of the year in 2010.

I share this story because I believe women want to run this kind of race. I believe women are told they can't win doing this, but clearly we have proven they can. And, Governor Pence chose me as his running mate, at least partially, because of this approach which we followed in 2012.

I believe that, if we are to raise the esteem of "politicians," we must be of highest integrity, both in our campaigns and in our public service. How we win is important. How we govern is even more important. The campaign is the prelude for how we will govern.

Our tenth commandment was that we would be proud of the race we ran the day after the election, win or lose. We were. I cannot imagine running, winning, or losing any other way.

—Indiana Lt. Governor Sue Ellspermann

Famous former Speaker of the House Tip O'Neill is credited with the phrase "All politics is local." President Lyndon Johnson is reported as believing "All politics is personal." Both are true. Everyday issues matter to voters and they trust you to help resolve them.

—Indiana State Rep. Gail Riecken

The best advice I can give from my own personal experience to a candidate is be personal. Sincerely listen to your constituents and in some way meet their need even on a small scale. I found people respected and remembered you more because you took the time to listen and do something. And always speak from the heart with passion and care.

—Karen L. Ragland, Evansville-Vanderburgh School Corporation Board of School Trustee, 2008–Present

---

Get a strong team to help you be grounded and stay focused during your campaign. There were two individuals who were extremely important to me when I ran for office. My scheduler was a life saver. Not only did she schedule my events but also she did all the research of activities and events I needed to be involved in during the campaign. The other person was my political and financial adviser. He assisted me with strategies to raise money and how to present myself as a political candidate. He had run and won many elections himself, so he had the experience from the inside out.

—Maura G. Robinson, MPA, author of *The Inclusion Revolution Is Now*

Tina E. Murphy, Ph.D., who ran for office in southwestern Indiana, offers the following advice to candidates:

- The only way you learn how to win is by running, first by helping many others in their campaigns and garnering support points, and then by choosing the office you wish to run for and the time to launch your campaign.
- You have to really "want it" more than anything else … deep down to the bone! For at least eighteen to twenty-four months, you must be eating, drinking, thinking about and dreaming of the campaign … laser focused 24/7.

- Immediately, create a 4–5 member trusted campaign team with a gifted, sage manager to help with the details.
- You must become comfortable asking for money. Without sufficient funds, your campaign will die.
- You must be serious minded, classy, smiling, approachable and gracious. A touch of humor is good.
- Perception *is* political reality. You are "on" from the moment you wake up until the moment you rest your head.
- Develop and hone in on One Central Message … a mantra in less than 3–4 sentences. Example, Barack Obama's message was Change. Stand for something, not just political Pablum!
- To get yourself into the eye of the voter, use every mode of communication that you can afford … radio, television, mailers, door hangers, e-mails, billboards, news ads, and especially door-to-door campaigning, as you make your win one vote at time.
- A campaign is a marathon, not a sprint. It has two peaks of energy focus: the primary and the general election. If you rest between them, you do so at your peril.
- There is *always* an element of luck in winning, as you can never control all the intervening variables. Your first campaign, you learn how to win; your second campaign, you must win; if you lose your second campaign too, your chances of being successful at a third run are greatly diminished.

  People who get appointed to serve a portion of a vacated term often lose because they do not understand all of the above.

Be fair and do what is right. I have found over the years that it does pay off. Even though I run on the Republican ticket, I have always gotten along well with the Democrats because I did do what was right and fair. Building a background like that helps any candidate when running for office. And … learn to disagree without being disagreeable.

—Susan K. Kirk, Vanderburgh County Treasurer

As a female candidate do not always expect you and your male counterparts will be asked the same question. Early in my political career I actually had someone say that they saw the picture of me with my small children and wanted to know who would be watching the children while I was campaigning and serving in elected office. I never heard anyone ask a man that question. I politely pointed out that they were my step sons and their mother actually took care of them except for the weekends when my husband and I had them with us. Evidently it did not harm them any. We ended up with a college professor, two engineers and two attorneys. The point is, it is there is still the stereotype that we as women cannot possibly handle certain jobs

—Marsha Abell, Vanderburgh County Commissioner

Politics requires passion, dedication and making sacrifices. We are held accountable by our constituents; thus, it is important to have a supportive circle of family and friends. To be successful in your campaign, you not only need a supportive circle but you also should have a well-organized plan. Most important tip of all, stay true to yourself. Now go forth and serve!

—Stephanie Terry, Vanderburgh County
Council, District 3 Member

Questions

1. Think back to the last several campaign seasons in your community. Did the way the women campaigned for office differ from the way their male counterparts did? In what ways?

2. Was there a difference in the way female candidates were covered in the local media?

3. Who is a female officeholder in your community that you admire? What do you remember about her campaigns? What does she do effectively that you would like to incorporate into your campaign?

Actions

1. Check with your local political party to see if there is a women's organization within the party that helps female candidates raise money.

2. Contact a female officeholder to see if you can meet for coffee to ask her for advice on running for office in your community.

CHAPTER 12

Putting It All Together

Deciding to run for office takes courage for you, the candidate, and for your family and close friends. It also takes considerable time, money, and personal sacrifice from you and your supporters. The time you invest up front to learn the political landscape of your community, to choose and develop your campaign team, and to plan how you'll raise funds to get your name and message out to voters will get you off to a solid start.

The more you prepare the more time you'll have to get out and meet voters and learn about the things you can do in local government to improve the quality of life for everyone in your community. And that's what it's all about—serving the people in your community to improve their quality of life.

I sincerely hope this book has given you tips to get started and to make the most of the journey.

Here are checklists that combine some of the main steps and basic information needed for your campaign. Complete these to keep you focused on your goal and on task.

Office I'm seeking: _____

Date of the election: _____

To win the race, I need at least _____ votes.

The office I'm running for is responsible for _____

_____

My 3 main goals to achieve once I am elected:

1) _____

2) _____

3) _____

My top qualifications for the office:

1) _____

2) _____

3) _____

I can give _____ hours per week to the campaign.

The main costs of my campaign will be:

1) _____

2) _____

3) _____

I need to raise $_____ for my campaign.

Dates of my fundraisers:

_____

_____

My campaign manager is _____

My treasurer is _____

Mailing address for contributions: _____

Main Steps to Launch Campaign

Below is a quick snapshot of the most basic steps to begin your campaign.

_____ 1) Formulate your message.
_____ 2) Build your campaign team.
_____ 3) Open a separate checking account for your campaign.
_____ 4) Establish your campaign budget.
_____ 5) Schedule your fundraisers.
_____ 6) Develop your campaign materials.

Checklist of People to Interview to Gain Information for Your Campaign

(This is a minimum. Depending on the office you are seeking, you'll want to expand this list to include community leaders and stakeholders who understand the issues your community faces.)

1) Chairs of the local political parties
2) Person who currently holds this office (if the person is not running for re-election)
3) Current officeholders you will be working with when you are elected
4) Officers of the neighborhood associations
5) President of the Chamber of Commerce

Resources

Here is a list of resources that can help you run your campaign.

- *The Campaign Manager: Running and Winning Local Elections* by Catherine Marie Shaw. This book is a thorough reference on the ins and outs of how to manage a campaign for a local candidate. It's great to read chapter by chapter, but if you're short on time, it's also a great reference book that includes a wealth of practical information, including sample campaign budgets, ad copy, and worksheets.
- U.S. Election Assistance Commission at www.eac.gov. Visit this website for the Quick State Election Info Cheat Sheet, which lists each state's polling place hours. You can also click your state on the map to visit your state government's election website. Use this to locate your community's polling places and other important election information from your state.
- National Association of Counties at www.naco.org.
- Go to www.governing.com, a website that has information on state and local government issues and ideas. Governing. com publishes the *Governing* magazine, a national monthly publication for leaders of state and local government.
- Project Vote Smart at www.votesmart.org. This nonpartisan and nonprofit organization provides a wealth of information

on national issues that you might find helpful as you develop your local campaign.

- Localvictory.com. This site provides advice on important topics for candidates in local races. You can sign up to receive a free weekly newsletter, which includes information on everything from raising funds for your campaign to ways to receive more free publicity.

Recommended Reading

Get Out the Vote: How to Increase Voter Turnout, 2nd edition, by Donald P. Green and Alan S. Gerber.

Additional Resources for Female Candidates

- She Should Run, an organization committed to increasing the number of women in public office. Contact them at 1900 L Street NW, Suite 500, Washington, DC 20036 or www.sheshouldrun.org.
- The Center for American Women and Politics, whose mission is to provide a better understanding about how to enhance women's participation and leadership in politics and government. The center offers education and outreach programs that address the underrepresentation of women in politics. The center is a unit of the Eagleton Institute of Politics at Rutgers, the State University of New Jersey. Visit the website at www.cawp.rutgers.edu.

Recommended Reading

1. *Pearls, Politics, and Power: How Women Can Win and Lead* by Madeleine M. Kunin, former three-term Vermont governor and ambassador to Switzerland. Gov. Kunin spoke at my community's Equality Day and shared her experiences

as a female governor. Her book shares what she has learned as a female candidate and officeholder.

2. Section titled "Who Gets Asked to Run for Office" in *It Takes a Candidate: Why Women Don't Run* by Jennifer L. Lawless and Richard L. Fox.

Open Book Editions
A Berrett-Koehler Partner

Open Book Editions is a joint venture between Berrett-Koehler Publishers and Author Solutions, the market leader in self-publishing. There are many more aspiring authors who share Berrett-Koehler's mission than we can sustainably publish. To serve these authors, Open Book Editions offers a comprehensive self-publishing opportunity.

A Shared Mission

Open Book Editions welcomes authors who share the Berrett-Koehler mission—Creating a World That Works for All. We believe that to truly create a better world, action is needed at all levels—individual, organizational, and societal. At the individual level, our publications help people align their lives with their values and with their aspirations for a better world. At the organizational level, we promote progressive leadership and management practices, socially responsible approaches to business, and humane and effective organizations. At the societal level, we publish content that advances social and economic justice, shared prosperity, sustainability, and new solutions to national and global issues.

Open Book Editions represents a new way to further the BK mission and expand our community. We look forward to helping more authors challenge conventional thinking, introduce new ideas, and foster positive change.

For more information, see the Open Book Editions website:
http://www.iuniverse.com/Packages/OpenBookEditions.aspx

Join the BK Community! See exclusive author videos, join discussion groups, find out about upcoming events, read author blogs, and much more! http://bkcommunity.com/